*Tao Te Ching: An Illustrated Journey*
© Frances Lincoln Limited 1999

Translation copyright © 1988 by Stephen Mitchell
Information about the paintings by Dr Stephen Little © Frances Lincoln 1999
Calligraphy by So Hing Bun © Frances Lincoln 1999
For photographic acknowledgements and copyright details, see below

This edition published in 2013 by
Frances Lincoln Limited, 74–77 White Lion Street
Islington, London N1 9PF
www.franceslincoln.com

British Library Cataloguing in Publication Data
available on request.

ISBN 978-0-7112-1278-7

Designed by Sophie Pelham
Set in Baker Signet

Printed in China

14 16 18 19 17 15 13

PHOTOGRAPHIC ACKNOWLEDGEMENTS
Photograph © The Art Institute of Chicago: Verses 39-40 (Robert C. Ross Foundation and Russell Tyson
Endowment, 1995.208), 48-49 (Kate S. Buckingham Endowment; restricted gift of Rhodes and Leona B.
Carpenter Foundation, 1996.432)
Asian Art Museum of San Francisco, The Avery Brundage Collection: Verses 8-9 (B66D19), 37-38
(Gift of Mrs. Mary Gary Harrison, B69D52)
© The Cleveland Museum of Art, 1998: Verse 20 (Leonard C. Hanna, Jr., Bequest, 1977.172)
Courtesy of the Freer Gallery of Art, Smithsonian Institution, Washington, D.C.: Verses 1-2, 21-22, 23-24, 78-79
Honolulu Academy of Arts: Verses 35-36 (Gift of Robert Allerton, 1958. 2474.1), 46-47 (Partial purchase, partial gift
of Mr. and Mrs. Mitchell B. Hutchinson, 1991. 6221.1), 61-62 (Gift of the Wilhelmina Tenney Fund, 1971. 3852.1),
67-68 (Gift of Mrs. Carter Galt, 1957. 2307.1)
Liaoning Provincial Museum, Shenyang: Verses 59-60
Courtesy of the Museum of Fine Arts, Boston: Verse 41 (Chinese and Japanese Special Fund), 69-70
(Francis Gardner Curtis Fund)
National Gallery of Canada, Ottawa: Verses 26-27 (purchased 1956)
National Palace Museum, Taipei, Taiwan, Republic of China: Endpapers, Title page, Verses 3-4, 12-13, 16, 33-34
The Nelson-Atkins Museum of Art, Kansas City, Missouri (purchase: Nelson Trust): Cover, Verses 17-19, 42-43,
50-51, 57-58, 65-66, 71-74, 75-77
Nezu Institute of Fine Arts, Tokyo: Verse 52
Palace Museum, Beijing: Verses 5-7, 10-11, 25, 29-30, 31-32, 44-45, 53-54. 63-64, 80-81
The Saint Louis Art Museum: Verses 14-15 (William K. Bixby Asian Art Fund, 97:1926)
Shanghai Museum: Verses 28, 55-56

# TAO
# TE
# CHING

## LAO TZU

### TRANSLATED BY
### Stephen Mitchell

### FRANCES LINCOLN

# FOREWORD

*Tao Te Ching* (pronounced, more or less, *Dow Deh Jing*) can be translated as *The Book of the Immanence of the Way* or *The Book of the Way and of How It Manifests Itself in the World* or, simply, *The Book of the Way*. Since it is already well known by its Chinese title, I have let that stand.

About Lao Tzu, its author, there is practically nothing to be said. He may have been an older contemporary of Confucius (551-479 B.C.E.) and may have held the position of archive-keeper in one of the petty kingdoms of the time. But all the information that has come down to us is highly suspect. Even the meaning of his name is uncertain (the most likely interpretations: "the Old Master" or, more picturesquely, "the Old Boy"). Like an Iroquois woodsman, he left no traces. All he left us is his book: the classic manual on the art of living, written in a style of gemlike lucidity, radiant with humour and grace and large-heartedness and deep wisdom: one of the wonders of the world.

People usually think of Lao Tzu as a hermit, a drop-out from society, dwelling serenely in some mountain hut, unvisited except perhaps by the occasional traveller arriving from a '60s joke to ask, "What is the meaning of life?" But it's clear from his teachings that he deeply cared about society, if society means the welfare of one's fellow human beings; his book is, among other things, a treatise on the art of government, whether of a country or of a child. The misperception may arise from his insistence on *wei wu wei*, literally "doing not-doing", which has been seen as passivity. Nothing could be further from the truth. A good athlete can enter a state of body-awareness in which the right stroke or the right movement happens by itself, effortlessly, without any interference of the conscious will. This is a paradigm for non-action: the purest and most effective form of action. The game plays the game; the poem writes the poem; we can't tell the dancer from the dance.

> Less and less do you need to force things,
> until finally you arrive at non-action.
> When nothing is done,
> nothing is left undone.

Nothing is done because the doer has wholeheartedly vanished into the deed; the fuel has been completely transformed into flame. This "nothing" is, in fact, everything. It happens when we trust the intelligence of the universe in the same way that an athlete or a dancer trusts the superior intelligence of the body. Hence Lao Tzu's emphasis on softness. Softness means the opposite of rigidity, and is synonymous with suppleness, adaptability, endurance. Anyone who has seen a tai ch'i or ai-kido master doing not-doing will know how powerful this softness is.

Lao Tzu's central figure is a man or woman whose life is in perfect harmony with the way things are. This is not an idea; it is a reality; I have seen it. The Master has mastered Nature; not in the sense of conquering it, but of becoming it. In surrendering to the Tao, in giving up all concepts, judgements and desires, her mind has grown naturally compassionate. She finds deep in her own experience the central truths of the art of living, which are paradoxical only on the surface: that the more truly solitary we are, the more compassionate we can be; the more we let go of what we love, the more present our love becomes; the clearer our insight into what is beyond good and evil, the more we can embody the good. Until finally she is able to say, in all humility, "I am the Tao, the Truth, the Life."

The teaching of the *Tao Te Ching* is moral in the deepest sense. Unencumbered by any concept of sin, the Master doesn't see evil as a force to resist, but simply as an opaqueness, a state of self-absorption which is in disharmony with the universal process, so that, as with a dirty window, the light can't shine through. This freedom from moral categories allows him his great compassion for the wicked and the selfish.

> Thus the Master is available to all people
> and doesn't reject anyone.
> He is ready to use all situations
> and doesn't waste anything.
> This is called embodying the light.
>
> What is a good man but a bad man's teacher?
> What is a bad man but a good man's job?
> If you don't understand this, you will get lost,
> however intelligent you are.
> It is the great secret.

The reader will notice that in the many passages where Lao Tzu describes the Master, I have used the pronoun "she" at least as often as "he". The Chinese language doesn't make this kind of distinction; in English we have to choose. But since we are all, potentially, the Master (since the Master is, essentially, us), I felt it would be untrue to present a male archetype, as other versions have, ironically, done. Ironically, because of all the great world religions the teaching of Lao Tzu is by far the most female. Of course, you should feel free, throughout the book, to substitute "he" for "she" or vice versa.

As to method: I worked from Paul Carus's literal version, which provides English equivalents (often very quaint ones) alongside each of the Chinese ideograms. I also consulted dozens of translations into English, German and French. But the most essential preparation for my work was a fourteen-year-long course of Zen training, which brought me face to face with Lao Tzu and his true disciples and heirs, the early Chinese Zen Masters.

With great poetry, the freest translation is sometimes the most faithful. "We must try its effect as an English poem," Dr Johnson said; "that is the way to judge of the merit of a translation". I have often been fairly literal – or as literal as one *can* be with such a subtle, kaleidoscopic book as the *Tao Te Ching*. But I have also paraphrased, expanded, contracted, interpreted, worked with the text, played with it, until it became embodied in a language that felt genuine to me. If I haven't always translated Lao Tzu's words, my intention has always been to translate his mind.

I

The tao that can be told
is not the eternal Tao.
The name that can be named
is not the eternal Name.

The unnamable is the eternally real.
Naming is the origin
of all particular things.

Free from desire, you realise the mystery.
Caught in desire, you see only the manifestations.

Yet mystery and manifestations
arise from the same source.
This source is called darkness.

Darkness within darkness.
The gateway to all understanding.

## 2

When people see some things as beautiful,
other things become ugly.
When people see some things as good,
other things become bad.

Being and non-being create each other.
Difficult and easy support each other.
Long and short define each other.
High and low depend on each other.
Before and after follow each other.

Therefore the Master
acts without doing anything
and teaches without saying anything.
Things arise and she lets them come;
things disappear and she lets them go.
She has but doesn't possess,
acts but doesn't expect.
When her work is done, she forgets it.
That is why it lasts forever.

章
二

### 3

If you overesteem great men,
people become powerless.
If you overvalue possessions,
people begin to steal.

The Master leads
by emptying people's minds
and filling their cores,
by weakening their ambition
and toughening their resolve.
He helps people lose everything
they know, everything they desire,
and creates confusion
in those who think that they know.

Practise not-doing,
and everything will fall into place.

### 4

The Tao is like a well:
used but never used up.
It is like the eternal void:
filled with infinite possibilities.

It is hidden but always present.
I don't know who gave birth to it.
It is older than God.

章
五

### 5

The Tao doesn't take sides;
it gives birth to both good and evil.
The Master doesn't take sides;
she welcomes both saints and sinners.

The Tao is like a bellows:
it is empty yet infinitely capable.
The more you use it, the more it produces;
the more you talk of it, the less you understand.

Hold on to the centre.

章
六

### 6

The Tao is called the Great Mother:
empty yet inexhaustible,
it gives birth to infinite worlds.

It is always present within you.
You can use it any way you want.

## 7

The Tao is infinite, eternal.
Why is it eternal?
It was never born;
thus it can never die.
Why is it infinite?
It has no desires for itself;
thus it is present for all beings.

The Master stays behind;
that is why she is ahead.
She is detached from all things;
that is why she is one with them.
Because she has let go of herself,
she is perfectly fulfilled.

章
七

## 8

The supreme good is like water,
which nourishes all things without trying to.
It is content with the low places that people disdain.
Thus it is like the Tao.

In dwelling, live close to the ground.
In thinking, keep to the simple.
In conflict, be fair and generous.
In governing, don't try to control.
In work, do what you enjoy.
In family life, be completely present.

When you are content to be simply yourself
and don't compare or compete,
everybody will respect you.

## 9

Fill your bowl to the brim
and it will spill.
Keep sharpening your knife
and it will blunt.
Chase after money and security
and your heart will never unclench.
Care about people's approval
and you will be their prisoner.

Do your work, then step back.
The only path to serenity.

## 10

Can you coax your mind from its wandering
and keep to the original oneness?
Can you let your body become
supple as a newborn child's?
Can you cleanse your inner vision
until you see nothing but the light?
Can you love people and lead them
without imposing your will?
Can you deal with the most vital matters
by letting events take their course?
Can you step back from your own mind
and thus understand all things?

Giving birth and nourishing,
having without possessing,
acting with no expectations,
leading and not trying to control:
this is the supreme virtue.

## 11

We join spokes together in a wheel,
but it is the centre hole
that makes the wagon move.

We shape clay into a pot,
but it is the emptiness inside
that holds whatever we want.

We hammer wood for a house,
but it is the inner space
that makes it livable.

We work with being,
but non-being is what we use.

12

Colours blind the eye.
Sounds deafen the ear.
Flavours numb the taste.
Thoughts weaken the mind.
Desires wither the heart.

The Master observes the world
but trusts his inner vision.
He allows things to come and go.
His heart is open as the sky.

13

Success is as dangerous as failure.
Hope is as hollow as fear.

What does it mean that success is as dangerous as failure?
Whether you go up the ladder or down it,
your position is shaky.
When you stand with your two feet on the ground,
you will always keep your balance.

What does it mean that hope is as hollow as fear?
Hope and fear are both phantoms
that arise from thinking of the self.
When we don't see the self as self,
what do we have to fear?

See the world as your self.
Have faith in the way things are.
Love the world as your self;
then you can care for all things.

14

Look, and it can't be seen.
Listen, and it can't be heard.
Reach, and it can't be grasped.

Above, it isn't bright.
Below, it isn't dark.
Seamless, unnamable,
it returns to the realm of nothing.
Form that includes all forms,
image without an image,
subtle, beyond all conception.

Approach it and there is no beginning;
follow it and there is no end.
You can't know it, but you can be it,
at ease in your own life.
Just realise where you come from:
this is the essence of wisdom.

## 15

The ancient Masters were profound and subtle.
Their wisdom was unfathomable.
There is no way to describe it;
all we can describe is their appearance.

They were careful
as someone crossing an iced-over stream.
Alert as a warrior in enemy territory.
Courteous as a guest.
Fluid as melting ice.
Shapable as a block of wood.
Receptive as a valley.
Clear as a glass of water.

Do you have the patience to wait
till your mud settles and the water is clear?
Can you remain unmoving
till the right action arises by itself?

The Master doesn't seek fulfilment.
Not seeking, not expecting,
she is present, and can welcome all things.

近風呈巧媚

泡露逞紅妍

## 16

Empty your mind of all thoughts.
Let your heart be at peace.
Watch the turmoil of beings,
but contemplate their return.

Each separate being in the universe
returns to the common source.
Returning to the source is serenity.

If you don't realise the source,
you stumble in confusion and sorrow.
When you realise where you come from,
you naturally become tolerant,
disinterested, amused,
kind-hearted as a grandmother,
dignified as a king.
Immersed in the wonder of the Tao,
you can deal with whatever life brings you,
and when death comes, you are ready.

## 17

When the Master governs, the people
are hardly aware that he exists.
Next best is a leader who is loved.
Next, one who is feared.
The worst is one who is despised.

If you don't trust the people,
you make them untrustworthy.

The Master doesn't talk, he acts.
When his work is done,
the people say, "Amazing:
we did it, all by ourselves!"

## 18

When the great Tao is forgotten,
goodness and piety appear.
When the body's intelligence declines,
cleverness and knowledge step forth.
When there is no peace in the family,
filial piety begins.
When the country falls into chaos,
patriotism is born.

## 19

Throw away holiness and wisdom,
and people will be a hundred times happier.
Throw away morality and justice,
and people will do the right thing.
Throw away industry and profit,
and there won't be any thieves.

If these three aren't enough,
just stay at the centre of the circle
and let all things take their course.

Stop thinking, and end your problems.
What difference between yes and no?
What difference between success and failure?
Must you value what others value,
avoid what others avoid?
How ridiculous!

Other people are excited,
as though they were at a parade.
I alone don't care,
I alone am expressionless,
like an infant before it can smile.

Other people have what they need;
I alone possess nothing.
I alone drift about,
like someone without a home.
I am like an idiot, my mind is so empty.

Other people are bright;
I alone am dark.
Other people are sharp;
I alone am dull.
Other people have a purpose;
I alone don't know.
I drift like a wave on the ocean,
I blow as aimless as the wind.

I am different from ordinary people.
I drink from the Great Mother's breasts.

The Master keeps her mind
always at one with the Tao;
that is what gives her her radiance.

The Tao is ungraspable.
How can her mind be at one with it?
Because she doesn't cling to ideas.

The Tao is dark and unfathomable.
How can it make her radiant?
Because she lets it.

Since before time and space were,
the Tao is.
It is beyond *is* and *is not*.
How do I know this is true?
I look inside myself and see.

If you want to become whole,
let yourself be partial.
If you want to become straight,
let yourself be crooked.
If you want to become full,
let yourself be empty.
If you want to be reborn,
let yourself die.
If you want to be given everything,
give everything up.

The Master, by residing in the Tao,
sets an example for all beings.
Because he doesn't display himself,
people can see his light.
Because he has nothing to prove,
people can trust his words.
Because he doesn't know who he is,
people recognise themselves in him.
Because he has no goal in mind,
everything he does succeeds.

When the ancient Masters said,
"If you want to be given everything,
give everything up,"
they weren't using empty phrases.
Only in being lived by the Tao
can you be truly yourself.

章 二十三

23

Express yourself completely,
then keep quiet.
Be like the forces of nature:
when it blows, there is only wind;
when it rains, there is only rain;
when the clouds pass, the sun shines through.

If you open yourself to the Tao,
you are at one with the Tao
and you can embody it completely.
If you open yourself to insight,
you are at one with insight
and you can use it completely.
If you open yourself to loss,
you are at one with loss
and you can accept it completely.

Open yourself to the Tao,
then trust your natural responses;
and everything will fall into place.

## 24

He who stands on tiptoe
doesn't stand firm.
He who rushes ahead
doesn't go far.
He who tries to shine
dims his own light.
He who defines himself
can't know who he really is.
He who has power over others
can't empower himself.
He who clings to his work
will create nothing that endures.

If you want to accord with the Tao,
just do your job, then let go.

There was something formless and perfect
before the universe was born.
It is serene. Empty.
Solitary. Unchanging.
Infinite. Eternally present.
It is the mother of the universe.
For lack of a better name,
I call it the Tao.

It flows through all things,
inside and outside, and returns
to the origin of all things.

The Tao is great.
The universe is great.
Earth is great.
Man is great.
These are the four great powers.

Man follows the earth.
Earth follows the universe.
The universe follows the Tao.
The Tao follows only itself.

章二十六

## 26

The heavy is the root of the light.
The unmoved is the source of all movement.

Thus the Master travels all day
without leaving home.
However splendid the views,
she stays serenely in herself.

Why should the lord of the country
flit about like a fool?
If you let yourself be blown to and fro,
you lose touch with your root.
If you let restlessness move you,
you lose touch with who you are.

章二十七

## 27

A good traveller has no fixed plans
and is not intent upon arriving.
A good artist lets his intuition
lead him wherever it wants.
A good scientist has freed himself of concepts
and keeps his mind open to what is.

Thus the Master is available to all people
and doesn't reject anyone.
He is ready to use all situations
and doesn't waste anything.
This is called embodying the light.

What is a good man but a bad man's teacher?
What is a bad man but a good man's job?
If you don't understand this, you will get lost,
however intelligent you are.
It is the great secret.

章二十八

Know the male,
yet keep to the female:
receive the world in your arms.
If you receive the world,
the Tao will never leave you
and you will be like a little child.

Know the white,
yet keep to the black:
be a pattern for the world.
If you are a pattern for the world,
the Tao will be strong inside you
and there will be nothing you can't do.

Know the personal,
yet keep to the impersonal:
accept the world as it is.
If you accept the world,
the Tao will be luminous inside you
and you will return to your primal self.

The world is formed from the void,
like utensils from a block of wood.
The Master knows the utensils,
yet keeps to the block:
thus she can use all things.

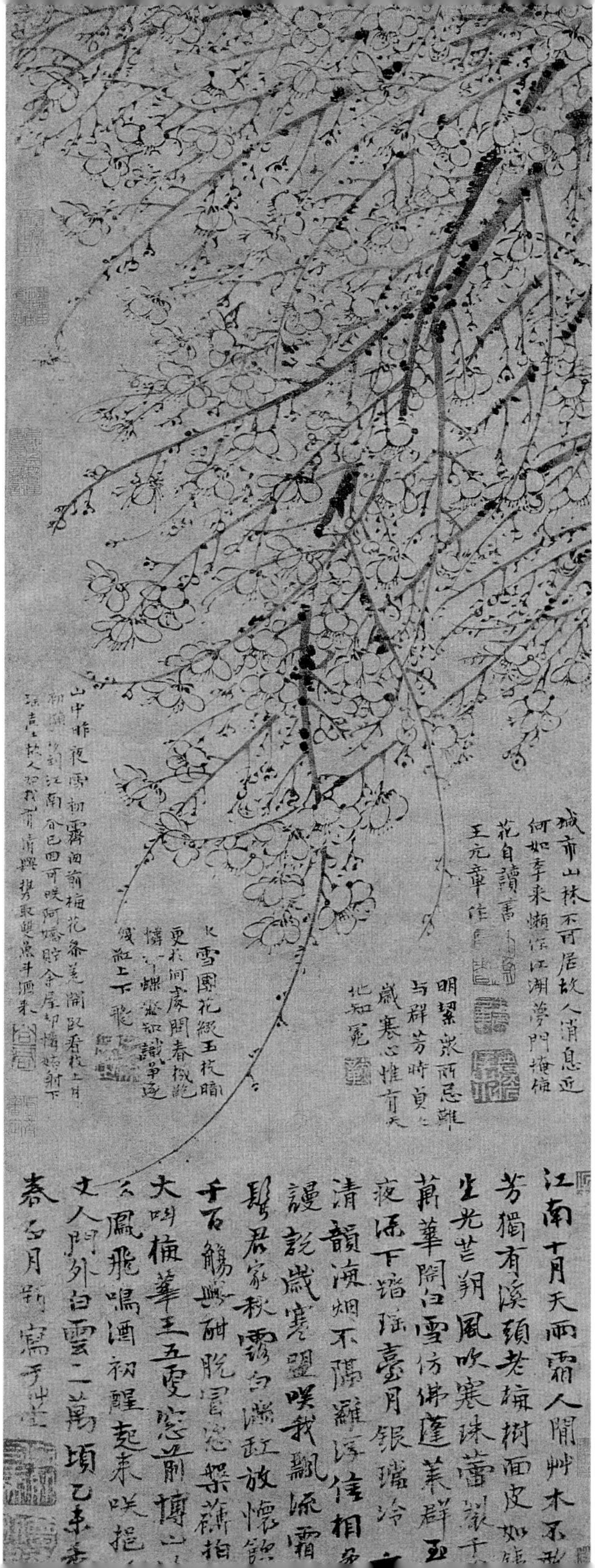

江南十月天雨霜　人間草木不敢芳
獨有溪頭老樹　面皮如鐵生光芒
翔風吹寒珠蕾千萬　葉開白雪
仿佛蓬萊群玉　夜深下瑤臺月銀瑠冷
清韻演煙不隨離浮佳相　謾說歲寒盟
嘆我飄流霜　聲君家秋露句瀉紅放懷餘
千百觴興酣脫冒寒架補　大叫梅華王
五更窗前博山久　鳳横鳴酒初醒起來咲
丈人門外白雲二萬頃　乙未春正月荊寫于此堂

城市山林不可居　故人消息近
何如李末顏渡江湖夢見梅
花自讀書
王元章作

明翠泉西忌雖
与群芳時頁
夜深
歲寒心推有天
地知寬

山中昨夜雨初
霽閣前梅花条
朔吹江南
己四可咲

火雪團花綴玉枝暗
更枝河庚開春城乾
情一蝶
幾紅上下飛

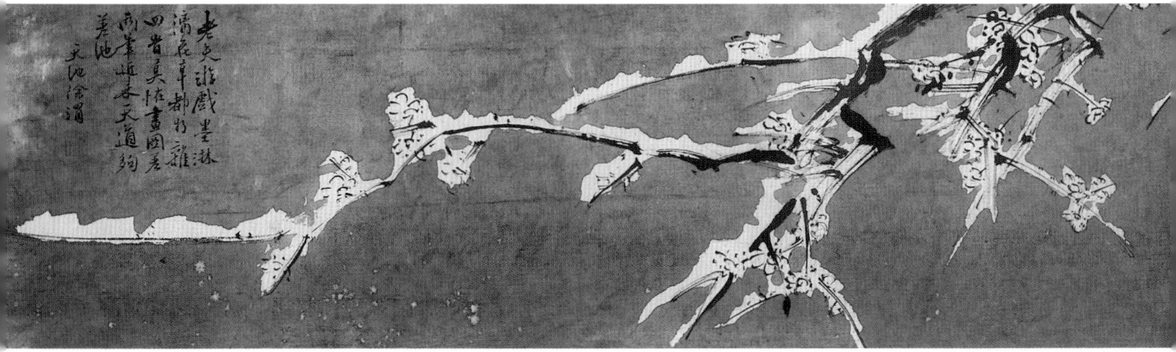

章二十九

29

Do you want to improve the world?
I don't think it can be done.

The world is sacred.
It can't be improved.
If you tamper with it, you'll ruin it.
If you treat it like an object, you'll lose it.

There is a time for being ahead,
a time for being behind;
a time for being in motion,
a time for being at rest;
a time for being vigorous,
a time for being exhausted;
a time for being safe,
a time for being in danger.

The Master sees things as they are,
without trying to control them.
She lets them go their own way,
and resides at the centre of the circle.

## 30

Whoever relies on the Tao in governing men
doesn't try to force issues
or defeat enemies by force of arms.
For every force there is a counterforce.
Violence, even well intentioned,
always rebounds upon oneself.

The Master does his job
and then stops.
He understands that the universe
is forever out of control,
and that trying to dominate events
goes against the current of the Tao.
Because he believes in himself,
he doesn't try to convince others.
Because he is content with himself,
he doesn't need others' approval.
Because he accepts himself,
the whole world accepts him.

Weapons are the tools of violence;
all decent men detest them.

Weapons are the tools of fear;
a decent man will avoid them
except in the direst necessity
and, if compelled, will use them
only with the utmost restraint.
Peace is his highest value.
If the peace has been shattered,
how can he be content?
His enemies are not demons,
but human beings like himself.
He doesn't wish them personal harm.
Nor does he rejoice in victory.
How could he rejoice in victory
and delight in the slaughter of men?

He enters a battle gravely,
with sorrow and with great compassion,
as if he were attending a funeral.

## 32

The Tao can't be perceived.
Smaller than an electron,
it contains uncountable galaxies.

If powerful men and women
could remain centred in the Tao,
all things would be in harmony.
The world would become a paradise.
All people would be at peace,
and the law would be written in their hearts.

When you have names and forms,
know that they are provisional.
When you have institutions,
know where their functions should end.
Knowing when to stop,
you can avoid any danger.

All things end in the Tao
as rivers flow into the sea.

## 33

Knowing others is intelligence;
knowing yourself is true wisdom.
Mastering others is strength;
mastering yourself is true power.

If you realise that you have enough,
you are truly rich.
If you stay in the centre
and embrace death with your whole heart,
you will endure forever.

## 34

The great Tao flows everywhere.
All things are born from it,
yet it doesn't create them.
It pours itself into its work,
yet it makes no claim.
It nourishes infinite worlds,
yet it doesn't hold on to them.
Since it is merged with all things
and hidden in their hearts,
it can be called humble.
Since all things vanish into it
and it alone endures,
it can be called great.
It isn't aware of its greatness;
thus it is truly great.

章
三
十
五

## 35

She who is centred in the Tao
can go where she wishes, without danger.
She perceives the universal harmony,
even amid great pain,
because she has found peace in her heart.

Music or the smell of good cooking
may make people stop and enjoy.
But words that point to the Tao
seem monotonous and without flavour.
When you look for it, there is nothing to see.
When you listen for it, there is nothing to hear.
When you use it, it is inexhaustible.

章
三
十
六

## 36

If you want to shrink something,
you must first allow it to expand.
If you want to get rid of something,
you must first allow it to flourish.
If you want to take something,
you must first allow it to be given.
This is called the subtle perception
of the way things are.

The soft overcomes the hard.
The slow overcomes the fast.
Let your workings remain a mystery.
Just show people the results.

吾家家坤
一府郎
寫竹閣

章
三
十
七

The Tao never does anything,
yet through it all things are done.

If powerful men and women
could centre themselves in it,
the whole world would be transformed
by itself, in its natural rhythms.
People would be content
with their simple, everyday lives,
in harmony, and free of desire.

When there is no desire,
all things are at peace.

38

The Master doesn't try to be powerful;
thus he is truly powerful.
The ordinary man keeps reaching for power;
thus he never has enough.

The Master does nothing,
yet he leaves nothing undone.
The ordinary man is always doing things,
yet many more are left to be done.

The kind man does something,
yet something remains undone.
The just man does something,
and leaves many things to be done.
The moral man does something,
and when no one responds
he rolls up his sleeves and uses force.

When the Tao is lost, there is goodness.
When goodness is lost, there is morality.
When morality is lost, there is ritual.
Ritual is the husk of true faith,
the beginning of chaos.

Therefore the Master concerns himself
with the depths and not the surface,
with the fruit and not the flower.
He has no will of his own.
He dwells in reality,
and lets all illusions go.

## 39

In harmony with the Tao,
the sky is clear and spacious,
the earth is solid and full,
all creatures flourish together,
content with the way they are,
endlessly repeating themselves,
endlessly renewed.

When man interferes with Tao,
the sky becomes filthy,
the earth becomes depleted,
the equilibrium crumbles,
creatures become extinct.

The Master views the parts with compassion,
because he understands the whole.
His constant practice is humility.
He doesn't glitter like a jewel
but lets himself be shaped by the Tao,
as rugged and common as a stone.

## 40

Return is the movement of the Tao.
Yielding is the way of the Tao.

All things are born of being.
Being is born of non-being.

## 41

When a superior man hears of the Tao,
he immediately begins to embody it.
When an average man hears of the Tao,
he half believes it, half doubts it.
When a foolish man hears of the Tao,
he laughs out loud.
If he didn't laugh,
it wouldn't be the Tao.

Thus it is said:
The path into the light seems dark,
the path forward seems to go back,
the direct path seems long,
true power seems weak,
true purity seems tarnished,
true steadfastness seems changeable,
true clarity seems obscure,
the greatest art seems unsophisticated,
the greatest love seems indifferent,
the greatest wisdom seems childish.

The Tao is nowhere to be found.
Yet it nourishes and completes all things.

## 42

The Tao gives birth to One.
One gives birth to Two.
Two gives birth to Three.
Three gives birth to all things.

All things have their backs to the female
and stand facing the male.
When male and female combine,
all things achieve harmony.

Ordinary men hate solitude.
But the Master makes use of it,
embracing his aloneness, realising
he is one with the whole universe.

## 43

The gentlest thing in the world
overcomes the hardest thing in the world.
That which has no substance
enters where there is no space.
This shows the value of non-action.

Teaching without words,
performing without actions:
that is the Master's way.

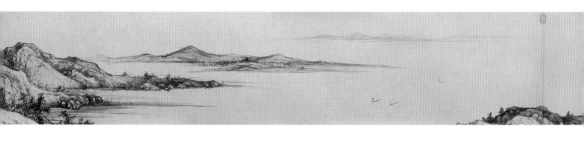

章
四
十
四

### 44

Fame or integrity: which is more important?
Money or happiness: which is more valuable?
Success or failure: which is more destructive?

If you look to others for fulfilment,
you will never truly be fulfilled.
If your happiness depends on money,
you will never be happy with yourself.

Be content with what you have;
rejoice in the way things are.
When you realise there is nothing lacking,
the whole world belongs to you.

### 45

True perfection seems imperfect,
yet it is perfectly itself.
True fullness seems empty,
yet it is fully present.

True straightness seems crooked.
True wisdom seems foolish.
True art seems artless.

The Master allows things to happen.
She shapes events as they come.
She steps out of the way
and lets the Tao speak for itself.

章
四
十
五

## 46

When a country is in harmony with the Tao,
the factories make trucks and tractors.
When a country goes counter to the Tao,
warheads are stockpiled outside the cities.

There is no greater illusion than fear,
no greater wrong than preparing to defend yourself,
no greater misfortune than having an enemy.

Whoever can see through all fear
will always be safe.

## 47

Without opening your door,
you can open your heart to the world.
Without looking out your window,
you can see the essence of the Tao.

The more you know,
the less you understand.

The Master arrives without leaving,
sees the light without looking,
achieves without doing a thing.

## 48

In the pursuit of knowledge,
every day something is added.
In the practice of the Tao,
every day something is dropped.
Less and less do you need to force things,
until finally you arrive at non-action.
When nothing is done,
nothing is left undone.

True mastery can be gained
by letting things go their own way.
It can't be gained by interfering.

## 49

The Master has no mind of her own.
She works with the mind of the people.

She is good to people who are good.
She is also good to people who aren't good.
This is true goodness.

She trusts people who are trustworthy.
She also trusts people who aren't trustworthy.
This is true trust.

The Master's mind is like space.
People don't understand her.
They look to her and wait.
She treats them like her own children.

## 50

The Master gives himself up
to whatever the moment brings.
He knows that he is going to die,
and he has nothing left to hold on to:
no illusions in his mind,
no resistances in his body.
He doesn't think about his actions;
they flow from the core of his being.
He holds nothing back from life;
therefore he is ready for death,
as a man is ready for sleep
after a good day's work.

## 51

Every being in the universe
is an expression of the Tao.
It springs into existence,
unconscious, perfect, free,
takes on a physical body,
lets circumstances complete it.
That is why every being
spontaneously honours the Tao.

The Tao gives birth to all beings,
nourishes them, maintains them,
cares for them, comforts them, protects them,
takes them back to itself,
creating without possessing,
acting without expecting,
guiding without interfering.
That is why love of the Tao
is in the very nature of things.

In the beginning was the Tao.
All things issue from it;
all things return to it.

To find the origin,
trace back the manifestations.
When you recognise the children
and find the mother,
you will be free of sorrow.

If you close your mind in judgements
and traffic with desires,
your heart will be troubled.
If you keep your mind from judging
and aren't led by the senses,
your heart will find peace.

Seeing into darkness is clarity.
Knowing how to yield is strength.
Use your own light
and return to the source of light.
This is called practising eternity.

山含秋色近
燕渡夕陽遲

醉公主

章
五
十
三

## 53

The great Way is easy,
yet people prefer the side paths.
Be aware when things are out of balance.
Stay centred within the Tao.

When rich speculators prosper
while farmers lose their land;
when government officials spend money
on weapons instead of cures;
when the upper class is extravagant and irresponsible
while the poor have nowhere to turn –
all this is robbery and chaos.
It is not in keeping with the Tao.

章
五
十
四

## 54

Whoever is planted in the Tao
will not be rooted up.
Whoever embraces the Tao
will not slip away.
Her name will be held in honour
from generation to generation.

Let the Tao be present in your life
and you will become genuine.
Let it be present in your family
and your family will flourish.
Let it be present in your country
and your country will be an example
to all countries in the world.
Let it be present in the universe
and the universe will sing.

How do I know this is true?
By looking inside myself.

55

He who is in harmony with the Tao
is like a newborn child.
Its bones are soft, its muscles are weak,
but its grip is powerful.
It doesn't know about the union
of male and female,
yet its penis can stand erect,
so intense is its vital power.
It can scream its head off all day,
yet it never becomes hoarse,
so complete is its harmony.

The Master's power is like this.
He lets all things come and go
effortlessly, without desire.
He never expects results;
thus he is never disappointed.
He is never disappointed;
thus his spirit never grows old.

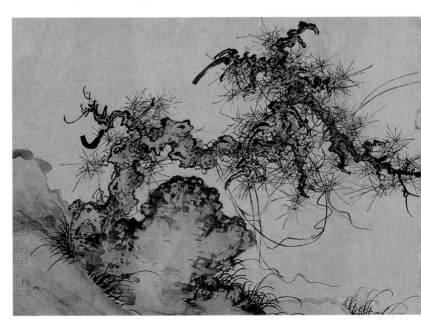

Those who know don't talk.
Those who talk don't know.

Close your mouth,
block off your senses,
blunt your sharpness,
untie your knots,
soften your glare,
settle your dust.
This is the primal identity.

Be like the Tao.
It can't be approached or withdrawn from,
benefited or harmed,
honoured or brought into disgrace.
It gives itself up continually.
That is why it endures.

章五十六

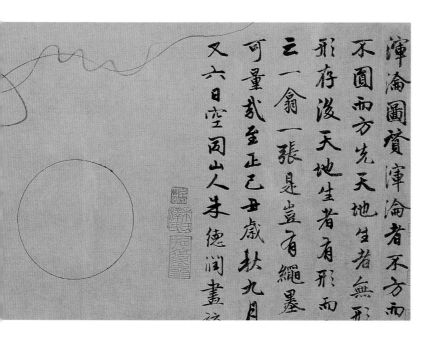

章
五
十
七

If you want to be a great leader,
you must learn to follow the Tao.
Stop trying to control.
Let go of fixed plans and concepts,
and the world will govern itself.

The more prohibitions you have,
the less virtuous people will be.
The more weapons you have,
the less secure people will be.
The more subsidies you have,
the less self-reliant people will be.

Therefore the Master says:
I let go of the law,
and people become honest.
I let go of economics,
and people become prosperous.
I let go of religion,
and people become serene.
I let go of all desire for the common good,
and the good becomes common as grass.

58

If a country is governed with tolerance,
the people are comfortable and honest.
If a country is governed with repression,
the people are depressed and crafty.

When the will to power is in charge,
the higher the ideals, the lower the results.
Try to make people happy,
and you lay the groundwork for misery.
Try to make people moral,
and you lay the groundwork for vice.

Thus the Master is content
to serve as an example
and not to impose her will.
She is pointed, but doesn't pierce.
Straightforward, but supple.
Radiant, but easy on the eyes.

章五十八

## 59

For governing a country well
there is nothing better than moderation.

The mark of a moderate man
is freedom from his own ideas.
Tolerant like the sky,
all-pervading like sunlight,
firm like a mountain,
supple like a tree in the wind,
he has no destination in view
and makes use of anything
life happens to bring his way.

Nothing is impossible for him.
Because he has let go,
he can care for the people's welfare
as a mother cares for her child.

## 60

Governing a large country
is like frying a small fish.
You spoil it with too much poking.

Centre your country in the Tao
and evil will have no power.
Not that it isn't there,
but you'll be able to step out of its way.

Give evil nothing to oppose
and it will disappear by itself.

## 61

When a country obtains great power,
it becomes like the sea:
all streams run downward into it.
The more powerful it grows,
the greater the need for humility.
Humility means trusting the Tao,
thus never needing to be defensive.

A great nation is like a great man:
When he makes a mistake, he realises it.
Having realised it, he admits it.
Having admitted it, he corrects it.
He considers those who point out his faults
as his most benevolent teachers.
He thinks of his enemy
as the shadow that he himself casts.

If a nation is centred in the Tao,
if it nourishes its own people
and doesn't meddle in the affairs of others,
it will be a light to all nations in the world.

## 62

The Tao is the centre of the universe,
the good man's treasure,
the bad man's refuge.

Honours can be bought with fine words,
respect can be won with good deeds;
but the Tao is beyond all value,
and no one can achieve it.

Thus, when a new leader is chosen,
don't offer to help him
with your wealth or your expertise.
Offer instead
to teach him about the Tao.

Why did the ancient Masters esteem the Tao?
Because, being one with the Tao,
when you seek, you find;
and when you make a mistake, you are forgiven.
That is why everybody loves it.

章六十三

Act without doing;
work without effort.
Think of the small as large
and the few as many.
Confront the difficult
while it is still easy;
accomplish the great task
by a series of small acts.

The Master never reaches for the great;
thus she achieves greatness.
When she runs into a difficulty,
she stops and gives herself to it.
She doesn't cling to her own comfort;
thus problems are no problem for her.

## 64

What is rooted is easy to nourish.
What is recent is easy to correct.
What is brittle is easy to break.
What is small is easy to scatter.

Prevent trouble before it arises.
Put things in order before they exist.
The giant pine tree
grows from a tiny sprout.
The journey of a thousand miles
starts from beneath your feet.

Rushing into action, you fail.
Trying to grasp things, you lose them.
Forcing a project to completion,
you ruin what was almost ripe.

Therefore the Master takes action
by letting things take their course.
He remains as calm
at the end as at the beginning.
He has nothing,
thus has nothing to lose.
What he desires is non-desire;
what he learns is to unlearn.
He simply reminds people
of who they have always been.
He cares about nothing but the Tao.
Thus he can care for all things.

章
六
十
五

## 65

The ancient Masters
didn't try to educate people,
but kindly taught them to not-know.

When they think that they know the answers,
people are difficult to guide.
When they know that they don't know,
people can find their own way.

If you want to learn how to govern,
avoid being clever or rich.
The simplest pattern is the clearest.
Content with an ordinary life,
you can show all people the way
back to their own true nature.

章
六
十
六

## 66

All streams flow to the sea
because it is lower than they are.
Humility gives it its power.

If you want to govern the people,
you must place yourself below them.
If you want to lead the people,
you must learn how to follow them.

The Master is above the people,
and no one feels oppressed.
She goes ahead of the people,
and no one feels manipulated.
The whole world is grateful to her.
Because she competes with no one,
no one can compete with her.

章六十七

67

Some say that my teaching is nonsense.
Others call it lofty but impractical.
But to those who have looked inside themselves,
this nonsense makes perfect sense.
And to those who put it into practice,
this loftiness has roots that go deep.

I have just three things to teach:
simplicity, patience, compassion.
These three are your greatest treasures.
Simple in actions and in thoughts,
you return to the source of being.
Patient with both friends and enemies,
you accord with the way things are.
Compassionate toward yourself,
you reconcile all beings in the world.

## 68

The best athlete
wants his opponent at his best.
The best general
enters the mind of his enemy.
The best businessman
serves the communal good.
The best leader
follows the will of the people.

All of them embody
the virtue of non-competition.
Not that they don't love to compete,
but they do it in the spirit of play.
In this they are like children
and in harmony with the Tao.

章六十八

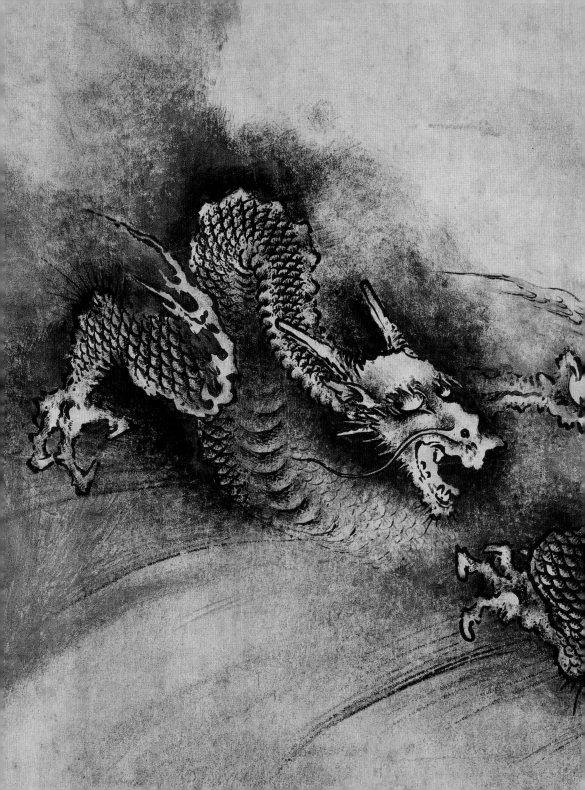

### 69

The generals have a saying:
"Rather than make the first move
it is better to wait and see.
Rather than advance an inch
it is better to retreat a yard."

This is called
going forward without advancing,
pushing back without using weapons.

There is no greater misfortune
than underestimating your enemy.
Underestimating your enemy
means thinking that he is evil.
Thus you destroy your three treasures
and become an enemy yourself.

When two great forces oppose each other,
the victory will go
to the one that knows how to yield.

### 70

My teachings are easy to understand
and easy to put into practice.
Yet your intellect will never grasp them,
and if you try to practise them, you'll fail.

My teachings are older than the world.
How can you grasp their meaning?

If you want to know me,
look inside your heart.

章七十一

### 71

Not-knowing is true knowledge.
Presuming to know is a disease.
First realise that you are sick;
then you can move toward health.

The Master is her own physician.
She has healed herself of all knowing.
Thus she is truly whole.

章七十二

### 72

When they lose their sense of awe,
people turn to religion.
When they no longer trust themselves,
they begin to depend on authority.

Therefore the Master steps back
so that people won't be confused.
He teaches without a teaching,
so that people will have nothing to learn.

### 73

The Tao is always at ease.
It overcomes without competing,
answers without speaking a word,
arrives without being summoned,
accomplishes without a plan.

Its net covers the whole universe.
And though its meshes are wide,
it doesn't let a thing slip through.

### 74

If you realise that all things change,
there is nothing you will try to hold on to.
If you aren't afraid of dying,
there is nothing you can't achieve.

Trying to control the future
is like trying to take the master carpenter's place.
When you handle the master carpenter's tools,
chances are that you'll cut your hand.

章七十五 章七十六

### 75

When taxes are too high,
people go hungry.
When the government is too intrusive,
people lose their spirit.

Act for the people's benefit.
Trust them; leave them alone.

### 76

Men are born soft and supple;
dead, they are stiff and hard.
Plants are born tender and pliant;
dead, they are brittle and dry.

Thus whoever is stiff and inflexible
is a disciple of death.
Whoever is soft and yielding
is a disciple of life.

The hard and stiff will be broken.
The soft and supple will prevail.

As it acts in the world, the Tao
is like the bending of a bow.
The top is bent downward;
the bottom is bent up.
It adjusts excess and deficiency
so that there is perfect balance.
It takes from what is too much
and gives to what isn't enough.

Those who try to control,
who use force to protect their power,
go against the direction of the Tao.
They take from those who don't have enough
and give to those who have far too much.

The Master can keep giving
because there is no end to her wealth.
She acts without expectation,
succeeds without taking credit,
and doesn't think that she is better
than anyone else.

章七十八

## 78

Nothing in the world
is as soft and yielding as water.
Yet for dissolving the hard and inflexible,
nothing can surpass it.

The soft overcomes the hard;
the gentle overcomes the rigid.
Everyone knows this is true,
but few can put it into practice.

Therefore the Master remains
serene in the midst of sorrow.
Evil cannot enter his heart.
Because he has given up helping,
he is people's greatest help.

True words seem paradoxical.

章七十九

## 79

Failure is an opportunity.
If you blame someone else,
there is no end to the blame.

Therefore the Master
fulfils her own obligations
and corrects her own mistakes.
She does what she needs to do
and demands nothing of others.

## 80

If a country is governed wisely,
its inhabitants will be content.
They enjoy the labour of their hands
and don't waste time inventing
labour-saving machines.
Since they dearly love their homes,
they aren't interested in travel.
There may be a few wagons and boats,
but these don't go anywhere.
There may be an arsenal of weapons,
but nobody ever uses them.
People enjoy their food,
take pleasure in being with their families,
spend weekends working in their gardens,
delight in the doings of the neighbourhood.
And even though the next country is so close
that people can hear its roosters crowing and its dogs barking,
they are content to die of old age
without ever having gone to see it.

## 81

True words aren't eloquent;
eloquent words aren't true.
Wise men don't need to prove their point;
men who need to prove their point aren't wise.

The Master has no possessions.
The more he does for others,
the happier he is.
The more he gives to others,
the wealthier he is.

The Tao nourishes by not forcing.
By not dominating, the Master leads.

# INFORMATION ABOUT THE PAINTINGS

Selecting the illustrations for this translation of the *Tao Te Ching* by Stephen Mitchell, I have aimed at a breadth of vision that resonates in some way with the directness and subtlety of the text. I have also tried to include something of the range of visual experience found in traditional Chinese paintings of the Sung (960-1279), Yüan (1260-1368), Ming (1368-1644), and Ch'ing (1644-1911) dynasties.

Adding a visual foil to the text, I am conscious of the extraordinary degree to which traditional Chinese painters and critics have articulated a belief that visual forms (*hsiang*) reveal the workings of the Tao. In recreating the forms of the world through painting, Chinese artists aimed to capture the inner essence of what they painted. This called for understanding: of the world, of oneself and of the means and techniques through which the artist mediated his experience. The goal of capturing the inner essence of what was being painted relied on a keen sympathy with the Tao that pervades the phenomenal world. As Kristofer Schipper has written, "The Tao is flux, transformation, process ('way') of alternation..." [1] This sensitivity to the presence of the Tao in the world is suggested by the great Northern Sung dynasty poet Su Shih (1037-1101), who wrote of his contemporary, the bamboo painter Wen T'ung:

> When Wen T'ung painted bamboo,
> He saw bamboo and not himself,
> Trance-like, he left his body behind.
> His body was transferred into bamboo,
> Creating inexhaustible freshness. [2]

On one level, the infinite transformations of the Tao are seen in the growth and decay of plants and flowers. Most plants in Chinese paintings, like bamboo, lotus, and blossoming plum, have a specific symbolism. Bamboo, for example, has long been associated with distinctly Taoist qualities: resilience and inner strength. Other plants, such as the lotus flower (a Hindu and Buddhist symbol of purity) are included here precisely because the Tao encompasses all things. As the *Tao Te Ching* states in verse 25:

> There was something formless and perfect
> before the universe was born.
> It is serene. Empty.
> Solitary. Unchanging.
> Infinite. Eternally present.
> It is the mother of the universe.
> For lack of a better name,
> I call it Tao.

The majority of the images in this book depict landscape. The finest Chinese landscape paintings convey both the outer forms of the world and the inner forces that give it shape. As early as the 5th century AD, the scholar Tsung Ping (375-443) wrote in his essay *Introduction to Painting Landscape*: "Sages, possessing the Tao, respond to things. The virtuous, purifying their thoughts, savour images. As for landscape, it has physical existence, yet tends toward the spiritual. Therefore, such recluses as the Yellow Emperor, Yao, Confucius, Kuang-ch'eng (a manifestation of Lao-tzu), Ta-k'uei, Hsü Yu and the brothers Po-i and Shu-ch'i from Ku-chu insisted upon roaming in the mountains K'ung-t'ung, Chu-tzü, Miao-ku, Chi, Shou, T'ai and Meng. These have also been praised as the pleasures of the humane and wise. Now, sages follow the Tao through their spirits, and the virtuous comprehend this. Landscapes display the beauty of the Tao through their forms, and humane men delight in this. Are these not similar?"[3]

The Chinese have traditionally believed that all natural phenomena (the seasons, for example) were caused by fluctuations in the cosmic balance of Yin and Yang, forces born of the Tao. Consciousness of this underlying duality and its machinations characterises much Chinese thought.

While the focus in most of the images is on the natural world, the human realm (including the political realm) is not left out. Qiu Ying's painting, *Emperor Kuang-wu of Han Fording a Stream* (v.26-27), which depicts a 1st-century emperor, widely admired for his moral integrity and for restoring Han rule after the reign of a usurper, is very much a visual paean to the type of sage-ruler described in the *Tao Te Ching*.

Several of the works illustrated here were painted by Taoists. The artists Tsou Fu-lei (v.1-2), Ni Tsan (v.48-49), Fang Ts'ung-i (v.53-54), and Emperor Hui-tsung (v.59-60) were all practising Taoists, and their paintings are imbued with a clarity of vision in keeping with the teachings of the *Tao Te Ching*. Other paintings are direct expressions of Taoist belief. Zhu Derun's handscroll entitled *Hunlun* (*Primordial Chaos*, v.55-56) symbolically depicts the emptiness that characterises the Tao itself, out of which primordial chaos and phenomenal reality emerge.

Finally, among the paintings featured are depictions of transcendents (immortals) and gods who play an important role in religious Taoism. Lü Tung-pin (v.17-19) is one of the 'Eight Immortals', and the patron saint of the Quanzhen (Complete Reality) school of Taoism, while the Taoist God of Earth is one of the Three Officials (San Kuan), deities who are judges of human fate (v.41). They are included here to emphasise that, regardless of the remarkable transformations that have occured in the history of religious Taoism (for example, the formation of a complex pantheon, and the critical role of alchemy in self-cultivation), the *Tao Te Ching* was always seen as the supreme expression of Taoist philosophy, and has always been at the centre of Taoist teaching and practise.[4]

FOOTNOTES

1. Kristofer Schipper (Karen C. Duval, trans.), *The Taoist Body* (Berkeley: University of California Press, 1993), p.4
2. Translated in Susan Bush & Hsio-yen Shih, *Early Chinese Texts on Painting* (Cambridge: Harvard University Press, 1985), p.212. Su Shih had an extensive knowledge of Taoism; see Farzeen Baldrian-Hussein, "Alchemy and Self-Cultivation in Literary Circles of the Northern Song Dynasty - Su Shih (1037-1101) and his Techniques of Survival," *Cahiers d'Extrême-Asie*, vol.9 (1996-7). pp.15-53
3. *Early Chinese Texts on Painting*, p.36
4. See the article by Livia Kohn on the *Tao Te Ching* in Taoist ritual in Livia Kohn & Michael LaFargue, eds., *Lao-tzu and the Tao-te-ching* (Albany: State University of New York Press, 1998)

# DETAILS OF THE PAINTINGS

**Cover and Verses 71-74:** Hsia Kuei (active c.1220-1250), *Twelve Views of Landscape*. Southern Sung dynasty, early-13th century. Handscroll; ink on silk. 28.0 x 230.8 cm.

**Endpapers:** Wu Chen, *Bamboo in Snow*. Yüan dynasty, dated 1350. Album leaf; ink on paper. 40.3 x 52 cm.

**Title page:** Chang Lu (c.1490-c.1563), *Lao-tzu Riding an Ox*. Ming dynasty, 16th century. Hanging scroll; ink and light colour on paper. 101.5 x 55.3 cm.

**Verses 1-2:** Tsou Fu-lei, *A Breath of Spring* (detail). Yüan dynasty, dated 1360. Handscroll; ink on paper. 34.1 x 223.4 cm.

**Verses 3-4:** Li Sung (active 1190-1264), *The Hang-chou Tidal Bore by Moonlight*. Southern Sung dynasty, early-13th century. Fan painting; ink and colours on silk. 22.3 x 22 cm.

**Verses 5-7 and 29-30:** Hsü Wei (1521-1593), *Flowers of the Four Seasons* (details). Ming dynasty, 16th century. Handscroll; ink on paper. 29.8 x 1090.6 cm.

**Verses 8-9:** Fan Ch'i (1616-1694), *Landscape* (detail). Ch'ing dynasty, dated 1645. Handscroll; ink and light colours on paper. 35.5 x 601.8 cm.

**Verses 10-11:** Ch'ien Ku (1508-1578), *Garden Grove after a Snowfall*, dated 1541. Ming dynasty. Hanging scroll; ink and colours on paper. 69.5 x 30.5 cm.

**Verses 12-13:** Emperor Hsüan-tsung (r.1426-1435), *Gibbons at Play*. Ming dynasty, dated 1427. Hanging scroll; ink and colours on paper. 162.3 x 127.7 cm.

**Verses 14-15:** Liu Ts'ai, *Fish Swimming Amid Falling Flowers* (detail). Northern Sung dynasty, early-12th century. Handscroll; ink and colours on silk. 26.8 x 252.2 cm.

**Verse 16:** Ma Yüan (active c.1160-after 1225), *Apricot Blossoms*. Southern Sung dynasty, early-13th century. Fan painting; ink and colours on silk. 25.8 x 27.3 cm.

**Verses 17-19:** Anonymous, *The Taoist Immortal Lü Tung-pin*. Yüan dynasty, 1260-1368. Hanging scroll; ink and colours on silk. 110.5 x 44.4 cm.

**Verse 20:** Wen Cheng-ming (1470-1559), *Listening to the Bamboo*. Ming dynasty, 16th century. Hanging scroll; ink on Sung dynasty sûtra paper. 94.5 x 30.5 cm.

**Verses 21-22:** Mao I (active c.1165-1173), *Swallows in a Willow Tree*. Southern Sung dynasty, late-12th century. Fan painting; ink on silk. 25.0 x 24.7 cm.

**Verses 23-24:** Anonymous, *Hills in Fog*. Yüan dynasty, 14th century. Handscroll; ink on paper. 24.9 x 92 cm.

**Verse 25:** Anonymous, *Lotus*. Southern Sung dynasty, 13th century. Fan painting; ink and colours on silk. 23.8 x 25.1 cm.

**Verses 26-27:** Ch'iu Ying (1510-1551), *The Emperor Kuang-wu Fording a River*. Ming dynasty, c.1540-1550. Hanging scroll; ink and colours on silk. 170.8 x 65.4 cm.

**Verse 28:** Wang Mian, *Branches of a Blossoming Plum*. Yüan dynasty, dated 1355. Hanging scroll; ink on paper. 67.7 x 25.9 cm.

**Verses 31-32:** Wang Hsi-meng, *A Thousand Li of Rivers and Mountains*, colophon by Ts'ai Ching dated 1113. Northern Sung dynasty, early-12th century. Section of a handscroll; ink and colour on silk. 51.5 x 119.1 cm.

**Verses 33-34:** T'ang Ti (c.1286-1354), *Travelling in the Autumn Mountains*. Yüan dynasty, 14th century. 151.9 x 103.7 cm.

**Verses 35-36:** Ch'ien Tu (1763-1844), *Landscape* (detail). Ch'ing dynasty, dated 1826. Fan painting; ink and light colours on mica-coated paper. 17.9 x 53.7 cm.

**Verses 37-38:** Sun K'o-hung (1532-1610), *The Stone Table Garden* (detail). Ming dynasty, dated 1572. Handscroll; ink and colours on paper. 31.1 x 370.8 cm.

**Verses 39-40:** Anonymous, *Dragon* (detail). Yüan dynasty, 14th century. Hanging scroll; ink and light colour on paper. 66.3 x 36.8 cm.

**Verse 41:** Anonymous (formerly attributed to Wu Tao-tzu), *Taoist Deity of Earth* (detail). Southern Sung dynasty, mid-12th century. Hanging scroll mounted as a panel; ink, colour and gold on silk. 125.5 x 55.9 cm.

**Verses 42-43:** Anonymous, *Fighting Birds on a Branch of Camellia*. Southern Sung dynasty, 1127-1279. Album leaf; ink and colour on silk. 23.5 x 26.8 cm.

**Verses 44-45:** Wang Fu (1362-1416) and Ch'en Shu-ch'i (14th - early-15th century), *Autumn Thoughts on the Hsiao and the Hsiang Rivers*. Ming dynasty, early-15th century. Handscroll; ink on paper. 25 x 569.5 cm.

**Verses 46-47:** Ch'ien Tu (1763-1844), *Immortal's Dwelling Among Plum Trees* (detail). Ch'ing dynasty, dated 1815. Hanging scroll; ink and colour on silk. 114.3 x 38.7 cm.

**Verses 48-49:** Ni Tsan (1306-1374), *Poetic Thoughts in a Forest Pavilion*. Ming dynasty, c.1371. Ink on paper. 124 x 50.5 cm.

**Verses 50-51:** Anonymous, *Fish and Water Grasses* (detail). Southern Sung dynasty, 13th century. Hanging scroll; ink on silk. 70.5 x 45.1 cm.

**Verse 52:** Ma Lin, *Sunset Landscape*, dated 1254. Southern Sung dynasty. Hanging scroll; ink and colour on silk. 51.5 x 27 cm.

**Verses 53-54:** Fang Ts'ung-i (c.1301-after 1378), *Rowing by Mt. Wu-i*. Yüan dynasty, dated 1359. Hanging scroll; ink on paper. 74.4 x 27.8 cm.

**Verses 55-56:** Zhu Derun (1294-1365), *Primordial Chaos*. Yüan dynasty, dated 1349. Handscroll; ink on paper. 29.7 x 86.2 cm.

**Verses 57-58:** Kung Hsien (1619-1689), *Landscape in the Manner of Tung Yüan*. Ch'ing dynasty, 17th century. Handscroll; ink on paper. 26.7 x 941.7 cm.

**Verses 59-60:** Emperor Hui-tsung, *Auspicious Cranes*. Northern Sung dynasty, early-12th century. Hanging scroll; ink and colour on silk. 1112.51 x 138.2 cm.

**Verses 61-62:** Anonymous, *Landscape* (detail). Ming dynasty, early-16th century. Handscroll; ink and silk. 24.4 x 352.1 cm.

**Verses 63-64:** Huang Ch'üan, *Sketches of Birds and Insects* (detail), c.960. Handscroll; ink and colour on silk. 41.5 x 70 cm.

**Verses 65-66:** Sheng Mou (active c. 1330-1369), *Enjoying Fresh Air in a Mountain Retreat* (detail). Yüan dynasty, 14th century. Hanging scroll; ink and colour on silk. 120.9 x 57.0 cm.

**Verses 67-68:** Wen Cheng-ming (1470-1559), *Landscape with Cypress and Waterfall*. Ming dynasty, c.1530-1545. Fan painting; ink and colours on gold-flecked paper. 17.8 x 51.5 cm.

**Verses 69-70:** Chen Jung (active first half of 13th century), *Nine Dragons* (detail). Southern Sung dynasty, dated 1244. Handscroll; ink and light colour on paper. 46.3 x 1096.4 cm.

**Verses 75-77:** Wang Fu (1362-1416), *Bamboo and Rocks* (detail). Ming dynasty, early-15th century. Handscroll; ink on paper. 35.5 x 232.5 cm.

**Verses 78-79:** Anonymous, *Boat Moored by a Stormy Lake*. Ming dynasty, 16th century. Fan painting; ink and colours on silk. 25.8 x 27.6 cm.

**Verses 80-81:** Sheng Mou (active c. 1330-1369), *Waiting for the Ferry on an Autumn River*. Yüan dynasty, dated 1351. Hanging scroll; ink on paper. 112.5 x 46.3 cm.